DK BIG BOOK OF
AIRPLANES

Caroline Bingham

A Dorling Kindersley Book

Dorling **DK** Kindersley

LONDON, NEW YORK, SYDNEY, DELHI, PARIS,
MUNICH, and JOHANNESBURG

Editor Caroline Bingham
Art Editor Susan Calver

Publishing Manager Sarah Phillips
Deputy Art Director Mark Richards
DTP Designer Megan Clayton
Jacket Designers Victoria Harvey
and Piers Tilbury
Picture Researcher Marie Osborn
Production Silvia La Greca
Photography Richard Leeney

First American Edition, 2001
06 10 9 8

Published in the United States by
Dorling Kindersley Publishing, Inc.
375 Hudson Street, New York, New York 10014

A CIP record is available from the Library of Congress

ISBN-13: 978-0-7894-6521-4

Color reproduction by Classicscan, Singapore
Pritned and bound in Singapore by Tien Wah Press

Dorling Kindersley would like to thank: Kristin Snow
at Air Tractor, Inc., Olney, Texas; Jack Brown's Seaplane Base, Florida;
Dan Sweet at Columbia Helicopters, Portland, Oregon; Major Mike Chapa
and John Haire at Edwards Air Force base, California; Fantasy of Flight,
Florida; Chris Finnigan, BMAA, Oxfordshire; Ellen Bendell at Lockheed
Martin, Palmdale, California; Beth Hagenauer at NASA Dryden Flight
Research Center, Edwards, California; Nancy Machado and
Duane Swing at Velocity Inc, Sebastian, Florida.

The publisher would like to thank the following for their
kind permission to reproduce their photographs:
Position key: c=center; b=bottom; l=left; r=right; t=top

Air Tractor inc: 10b. Austin Brown/Aviation Picture
Library: 3bl1, 20-21, 20-21b, 21tr. Donald Browning: 4tl.
Columbia Helicopters: 24tl. Edwards Airforce Base/Tom
Reynolds: 28bl. E.J. Koningsveld: 14tl, 14-15. Sipa Press/Chesnot:
20tl. N.A.S.A.: 2cl, 7bl, 16tl, 17cr, 22tl, 30tl, 30bl, 30-31, 31tr.
Plane Picture Company: John M. Dibbs 3tl, 14c, 15t.
Quadrant Picture Library: Chris Bennett 15br. Skyscan: Richard
Meredith-Hardy 18tl. Trh Pictures: 2-3t, 8-9t. Velocity Inc: 13br.

see our complete
catalog at
www.dk.com

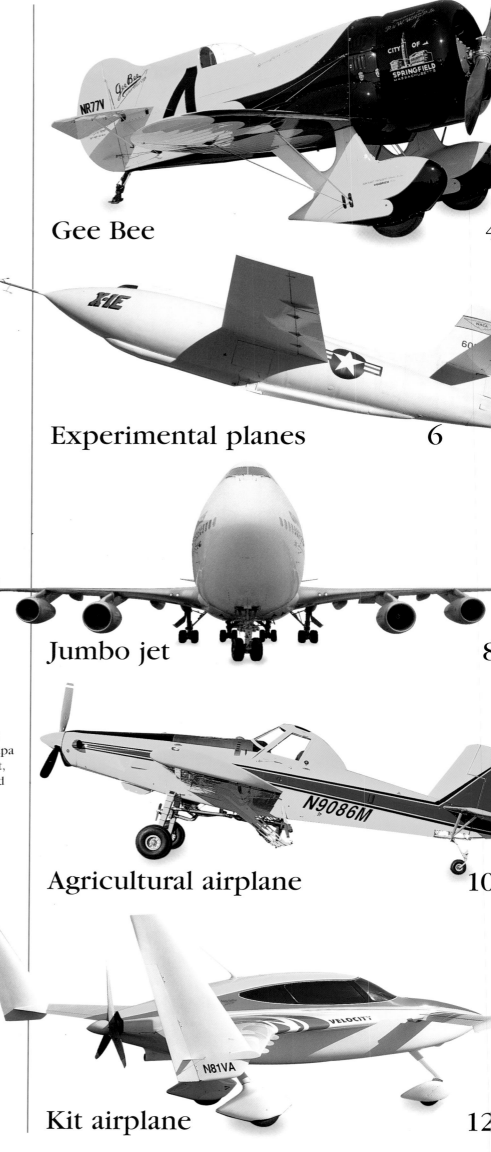

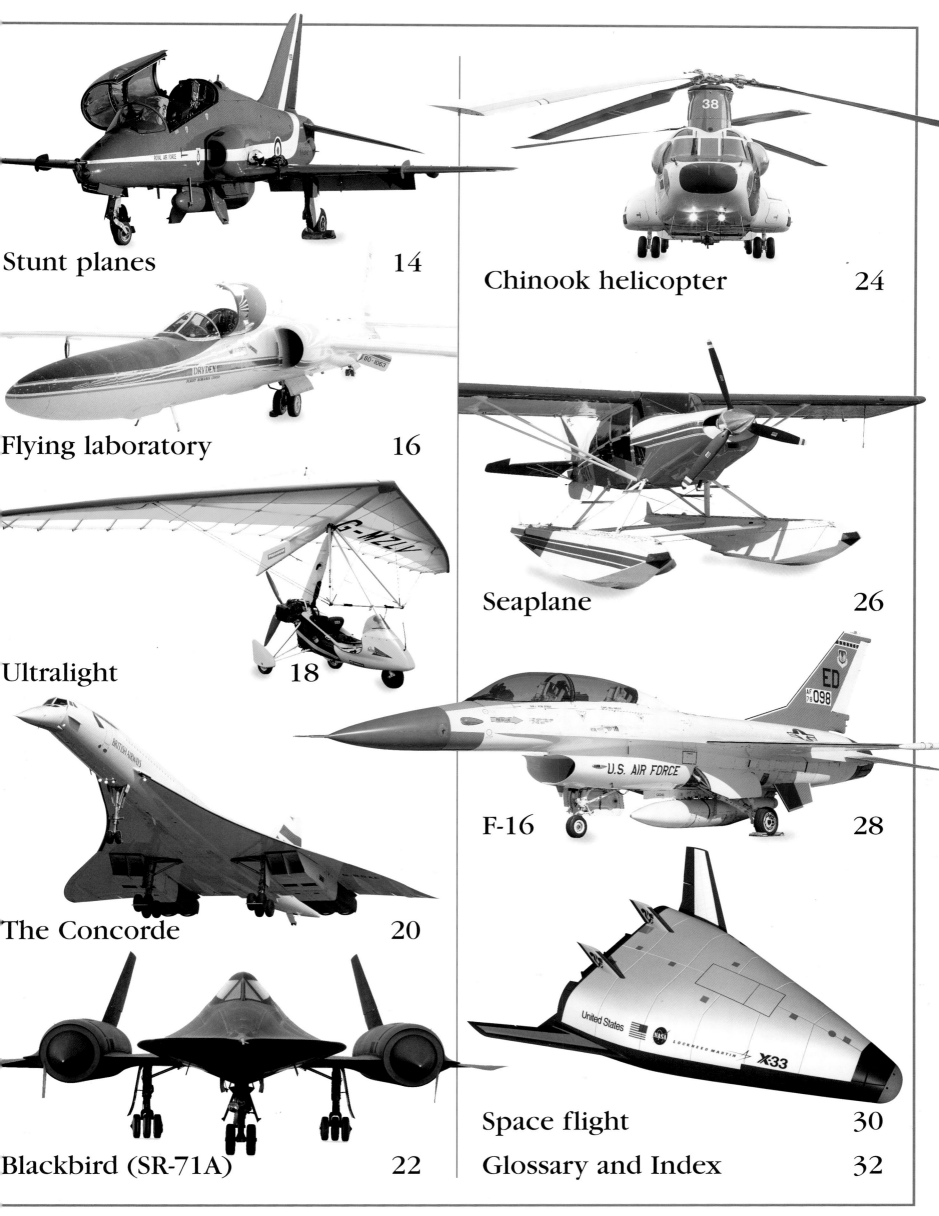

Gee Bee

Take a massive engine, add a pair of unusually short wings, and allow a tiny space for the pilot's cockpit. The result will probably look something like the spectacular Gee Bee Super Sportster, a plane that thrilled air-racing crowds in 1930s America with its extraordinary speed and daredevil tactics.

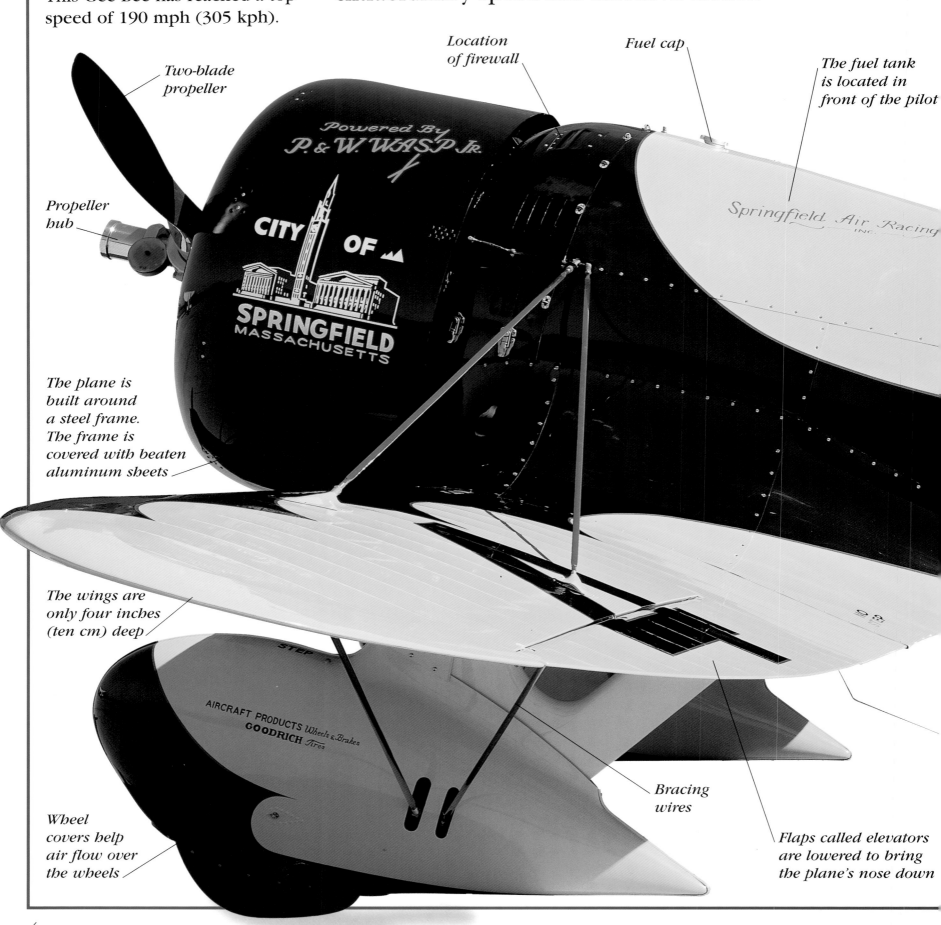

This Gee Bee has reached a top speed of 190 mph (305 kph).

Two-blade propeller

Propeller hub

Location of firewall

Fuel cap

The fuel tank is located in front of the pilot

The plane is built around a steel frame. The frame is covered with beaten aluminum sheets

The wings are only four inches (ten cm) deep

Bracing wires

Wheel covers help air flow over the wheels

Flaps called elevators are lowered to bring the plane's nose down

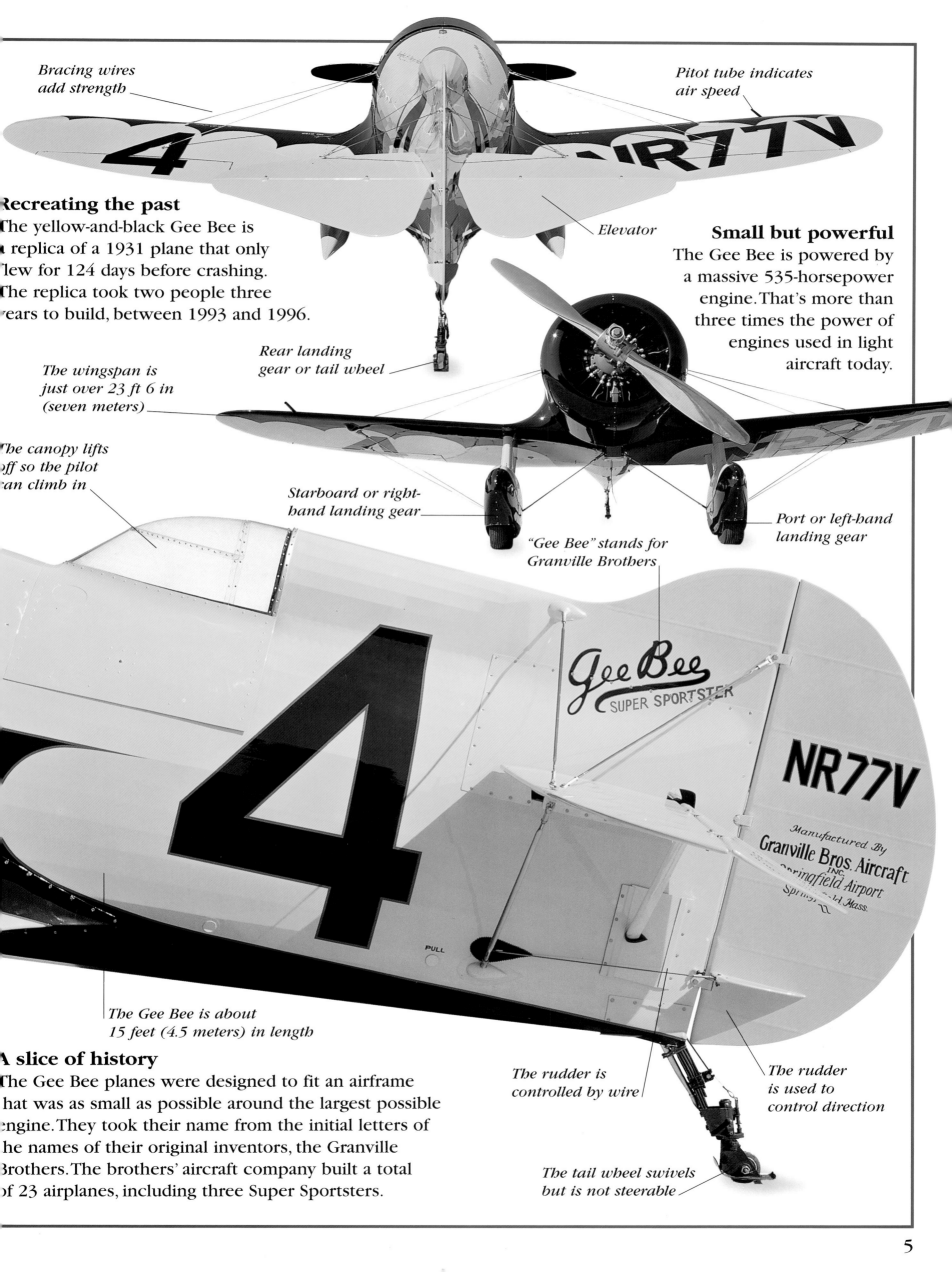

Bracing wires add strength

Pitot tube indicates air speed

Recreating the past
The yellow-and-black Gee Bee is a replica of a 1931 plane that only flew for 124 days before crashing. The replica took two people three years to build, between 1993 and 1996.

Elevator

Small but powerful
The Gee Bee is powered by a massive 535-horsepower engine. That's more than three times the power of engines used in light aircraft today.

Rear landing gear or tail wheel

The wingspan is just over 23 ft 6 in (seven meters)

The canopy lifts off so the pilot can climb in

Starboard or right-hand landing gear

"Gee Bee" stands for Granville Brothers

Port or left-hand landing gear

Gee Bee
SUPER SPORTSTER

NR77V

Manufactured By
Granville Bros. Aircraft INC.
Springfield Airport
Springfield Mass.

The Gee Bee is about 15 feet (4.5 meters) in length

A slice of history
The Gee Bee planes were designed to fit an airframe that was as small as possible around the largest possible engine. They took their name from the initial letters of the names of their original inventors, the Granville Brothers. The brothers' aircraft company built a total of 23 airplanes, including three Super Sportsters.

The rudder is controlled by wire

The rudder is used to control direction

PULL

The tail wheel swivels but is not steerable

Experimental planes

Fifty years ago the speed of sound was seen as a huge invisible barrier to the speed at which an airplane could fly. Planes that flew too near to this speed broke up after terrible buffeting. This changed with the X-planes, an experimental series of aircraft built to break all previous speed and altitude records.

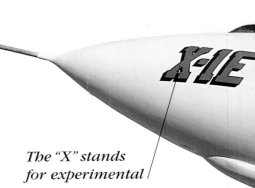

The "X" stands for experimental

Wedge-shaped tail

This X-15 is a replica. The original that carried this tail number crashed

The X-15 is 50 feet (just over 15 meters) long

A black dart

The X-15 is an incredible plane. Three X-15s made a total of 199 flights between 1959 and 1968. The fastest recorded speed was an astounding 4,520 mph (7,278 kph). It is the fastest rocket plane ever.

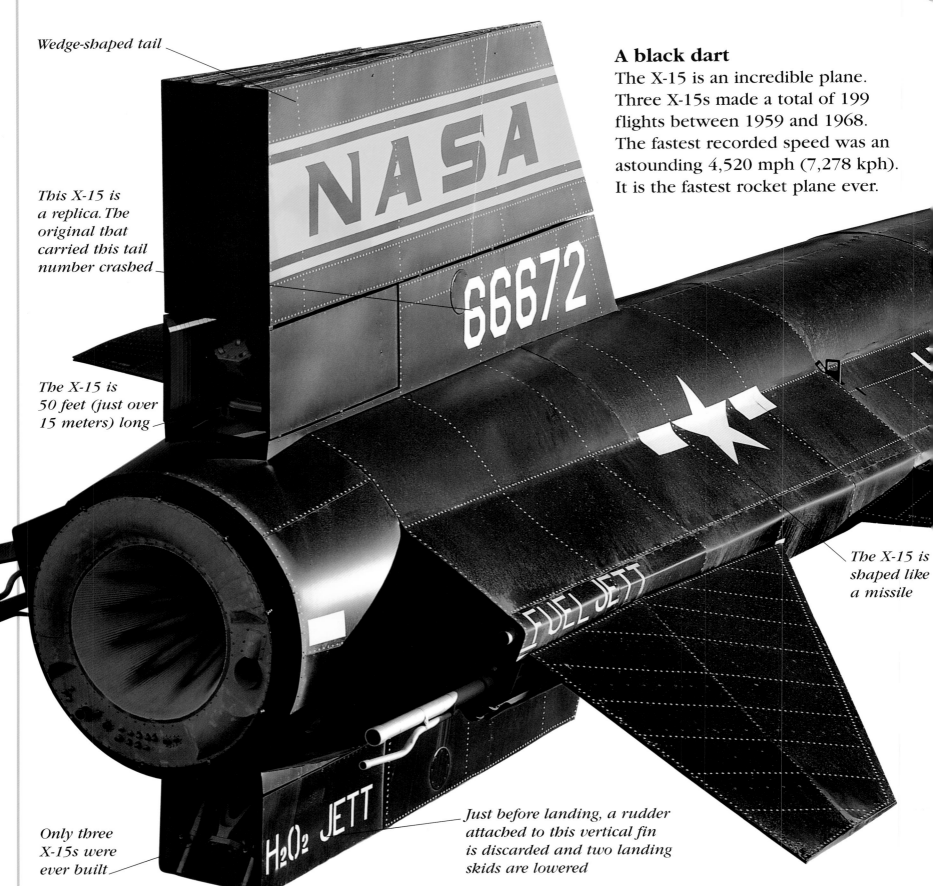

The X-15 is shaped like a missile

Only three X-15s were ever built

Just before landing, a rudder attached to this vertical fin is discarded and two landing skids are lowered

There are 343 gauges in the wings to measure different effects of speed

Faster than a bullet?

This plane, the X-1E, is an adapted version of the X-1, the first plane to break the sound barrier. The X-1 planes were deliberately shaped to resemble bullets. As the X-1 this plane first flew in 1946 – it was modified in 1955 and renamed the X-1E.

The X-1E is 31 feet (9.45 meters) long

There is only room for one pilot

In flight, the landing gear is contained beneath landing gear doors under the wings

More than half the plane's weight is taken up by fuel

X-1E

The speed of sound varies depending on altitude. The X-1E reached 1,471 mph (2,367 kph) at 73,458 feet (22,390 meters), more than twice the speed of sound at that height.

The X-1E is ten feet (three meters) high

A special metal skin withstood the high temperatures of hypersonic flight

The high-speed wing is only 3⅜ in (8.5 cm) thick

Four-chambered rocket engine

The wings are short and stubby

On one flight the X-15 reached an altitude of 67 miles (108 km) – the first manned flight into space!

X-15

The rocket engine was only used for the first 80-120 seconds of the X-15's flight. The rest of the flight was without power.

A massive rocket engine pushed the plane to travel 6,000 feet (1,829 meters) per second

The X-1E and X-15 were launched from the wing of a larger plane.

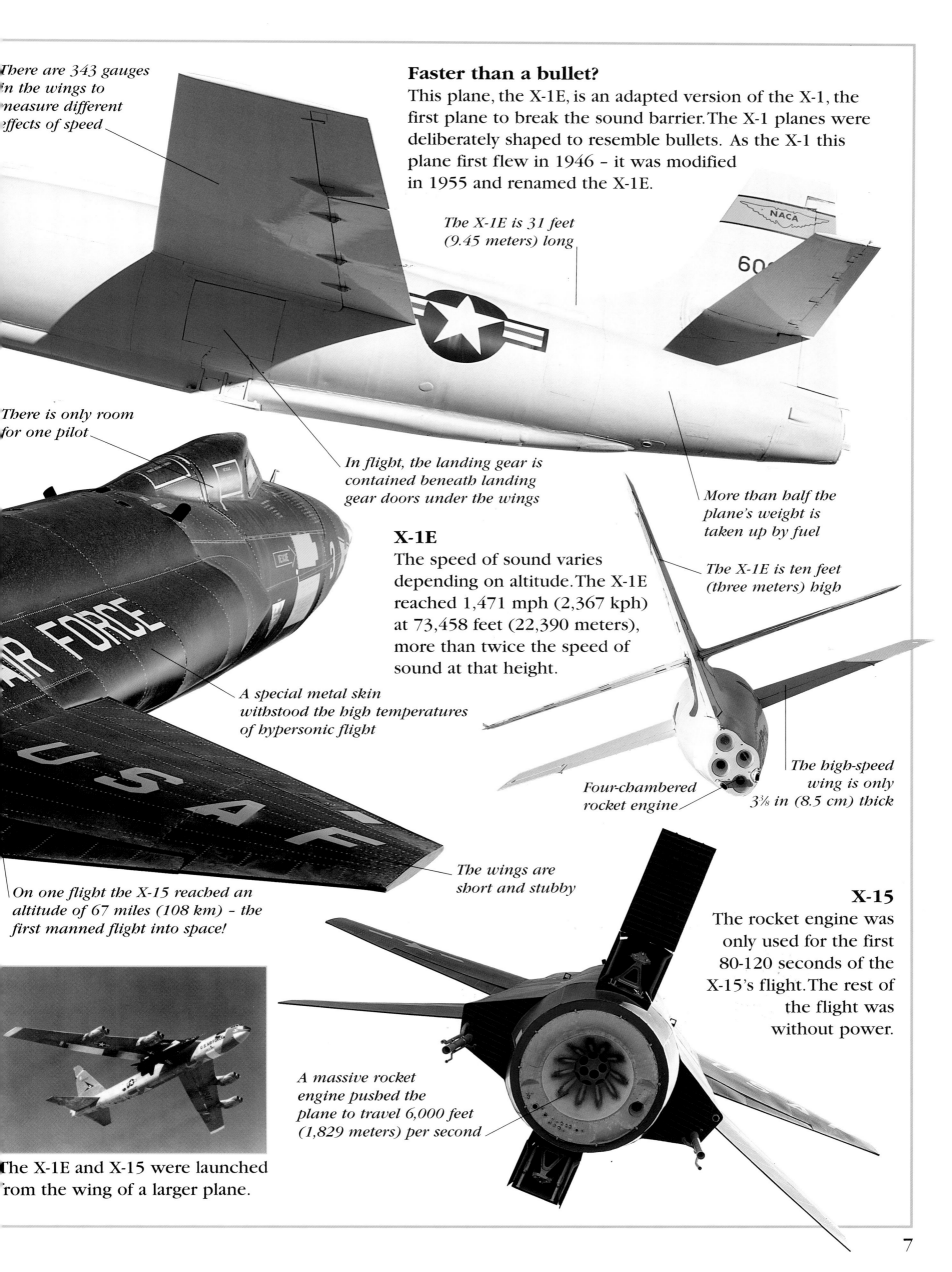

7

Jumbo jet

The Boeing 747 is currently the largest of all airliners. That is why it is also known as the jumbo jet. After its introduction in 1969, it doubled the number of passengers that could be taken on one airplane. Most jumbos seat 420 passengers, but some have an internal layout that allows them to carry 569 passengers!

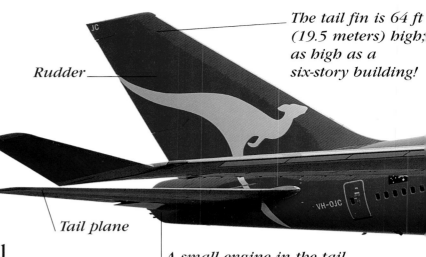

Rudder

The tail fin is 64 ft (19.5 meters) high, as high as a six-story building!

Tail plane

A small engine in the tail powers the jumbo's electrical and air-conditioning systems when on the ground

Talking big

The jumbo jet has a massive 196-ft (60-meter) wingspan and a fuselage wide enough to seat ten passengers side by side – with space for two aisles. The passengers may be on board for 11 hours, so the plane will be loaded with more than 800 meals and about 30 gallons (120 liters) of juice and water. Everything about the plane is big!

Multi-purpose plane

The jumbo jet has been modified to perform a number of different tasks. Two jumbos have been adapted to ferry a NASA Space Shuttle to and from its launch site. They have been strengthened and have large struts to support the shuttle.

The fuselage wall is 7.5 in (19 cm) thick and includes a layer of sound and heat insulation

In flight the winglet is angled downward, helping to direct air flow at the end of the wing

A wing's upper surface is curved more than its lower surface. As the engines push the plane forward, air rushing over the wings creates lift

The four engines are attached to the lower side of the wings

An adult could stand up in the engine air intake

A jumbo jet's landing gear is tested to support double the weight of the jet

Each tire is four feet (1.25 meters) in diameter

Exterior paint adds about 595 lb (270 kg) to the weight of a jumbo jet

Upper passenger deck

Toilet waste is stored in large tanks in the belly of the fuselage

There are a total of 18 wheels

Baggage holds are located in the bottom of the fuselage

Passenger door

Going the distance
A jumbo jet can travel a third of the way around the world without having to stop and refuel. It carries 56,420 gallons (217,000 liters) of fuel in seven tanks – three located in each wing and one in the center section between them.

Just like a car, a plane needs windshield wipers

The nose contains radar, which warns of obstacles around the aircraft – such as other planes, or an approaching storm

From bolts to wheels, there are about six million parts in a jumbo jet

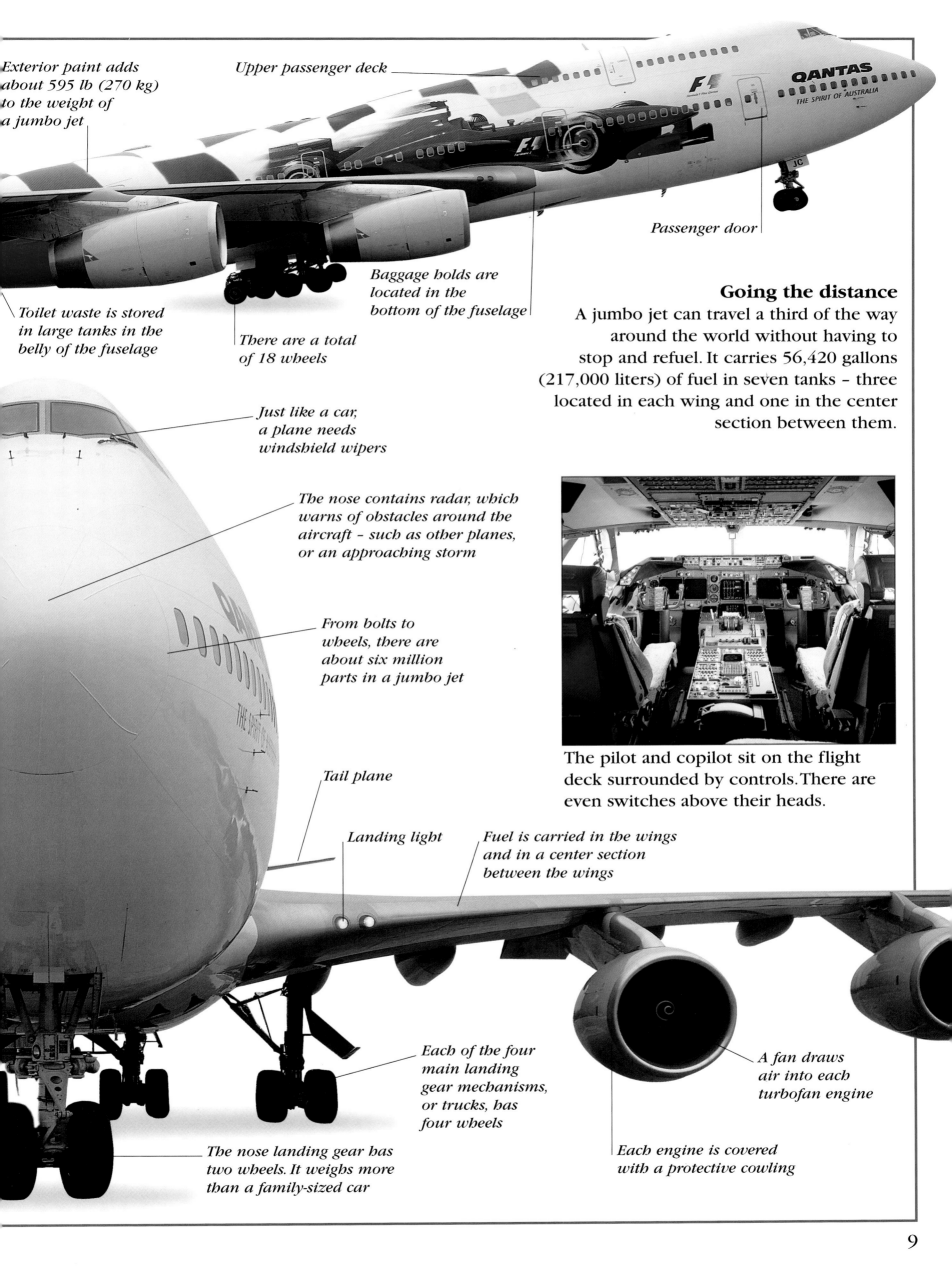

The pilot and copilot sit on the flight deck surrounded by controls. There are even switches above their heads.

Tail plane

Landing light

Fuel is carried in the wings and in a center section between the wings

Each of the four main landing gear mechanisms, or trucks, has four wheels

A fan draws air into each turbofan engine

The nose landing gear has two wheels. It weighs more than a family-sized car

Each engine is covered with a protective cowling

9

Agricultural airplane

Some farmers spray their crops to prevent damage from pests or to fertilize the crops to help them grow. They may be growing corn, or peanuts, or cotton. A quick way of doing this is to use a plane: a type of aircraft known as a cropduster will swoop low over a field and spray a crop in minutes.

The white tip makes a white ring when the propeller spins, making it easier to see!

An unusual feature of this plane is that the propeller can be used to allow the plane to reverse when taxiing on the ground

The plane's single 750-horsepower engine is located behind the propeller

Engine exhaust

The propeller makes 2,000 revolutions (turns) each minute

Each wing is six foot (almost two meters) wide

Fuel is carried in the wings

Metal struts, known as boom hangars, support the spray boom

Air leaving the wings creates a downwash that forces the spray to cover both the top and the bottom of the crop's leaves.

Air intake for engine

The landing gear is fixed and doesn't retract in flight

The pump that feeds the liquid product to the boom is turned by air flowing into this propeller

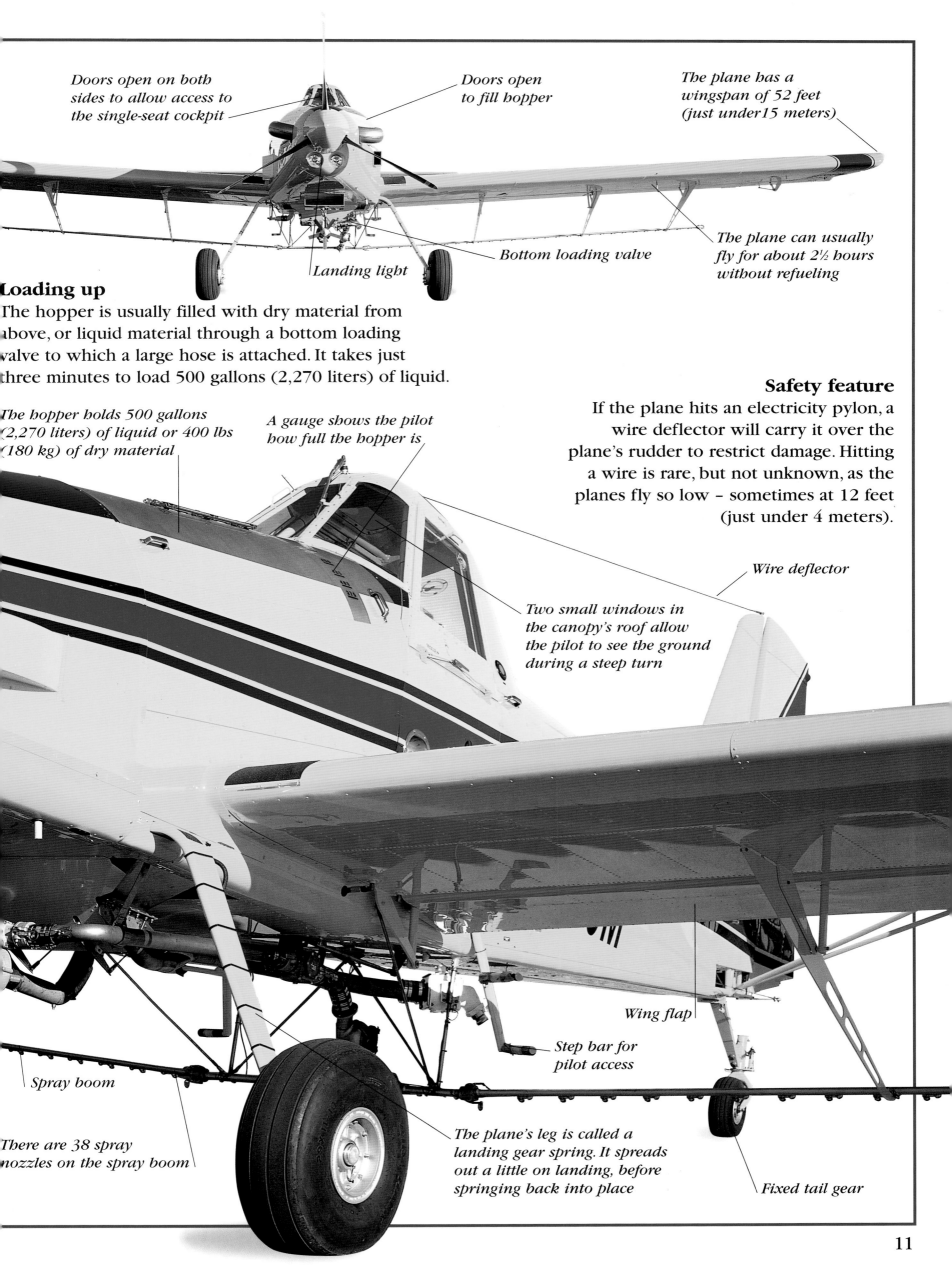

Doors open on both sides to allow access to the single-seat cockpit

Doors open to fill hopper

The plane has a wingspan of 52 feet (just under 15 meters)

Bottom loading valve

The plane can usually fly for about 2½ hours without refueling

Landing light

Loading up

The hopper is usually filled with dry material from above, or liquid material through a bottom loading valve to which a large hose is attached. It takes just three minutes to load 500 gallons (2,270 liters) of liquid.

Safety feature

If the plane hits an electricity pylon, a wire deflector will carry it over the plane's rudder to restrict damage. Hitting a wire is rare, but not unknown, as the planes fly so low – sometimes at 12 feet (just under 4 meters).

The hopper holds 500 gallons (2,270 liters) of liquid or 400 lbs (180 kg) of dry material

A gauge shows the pilot how full the hopper is

Wire deflector

Two small windows in the canopy's roof allow the pilot to see the ground during a steep turn

Wing flap

Step bar for pilot access

Spray boom

There are 38 spray nozzles on the spray boom

The plane's leg is called a landing gear spring. It spreads out a little on landing, before springing back into place

Fixed tail gear

Kit airplane

Imagine buying a kit and building your own airplane in a large garage! You could put together a plane like the Velocity, an eye-catching four-seater that looks very different than most light aircraft in the skies today.

The winglet helps lift the aircraft and acts as a vertical stabilizer

Fuselage

Tires

The single gull-wing door opens upward

The build-a-plane kits come with all the necessary nuts, bolts, and screws

One big jig-saw puzzle
This Velocity kit takes about 1,200 hours to build. That's the same as working a five-day week for 34 weeks.

Pitot tube

The fiberglass body is so light that an adult can lift the nose off the ground

Small wings at the front, called canards, help to lift the aircraft

Step to aid access to cabin

The plane seats four people including the pilot. It can carry about 600 lbs (272 kg) in weight of passengers and luggage

Nose wheel

Why is it white?
Under the fiberglass surface is a lightweight core material that shrinks in excessive heat. A white surface doesn't absorb as much heat as a dark surface, which means that the core material is not as likely to get so hot that it shrinks

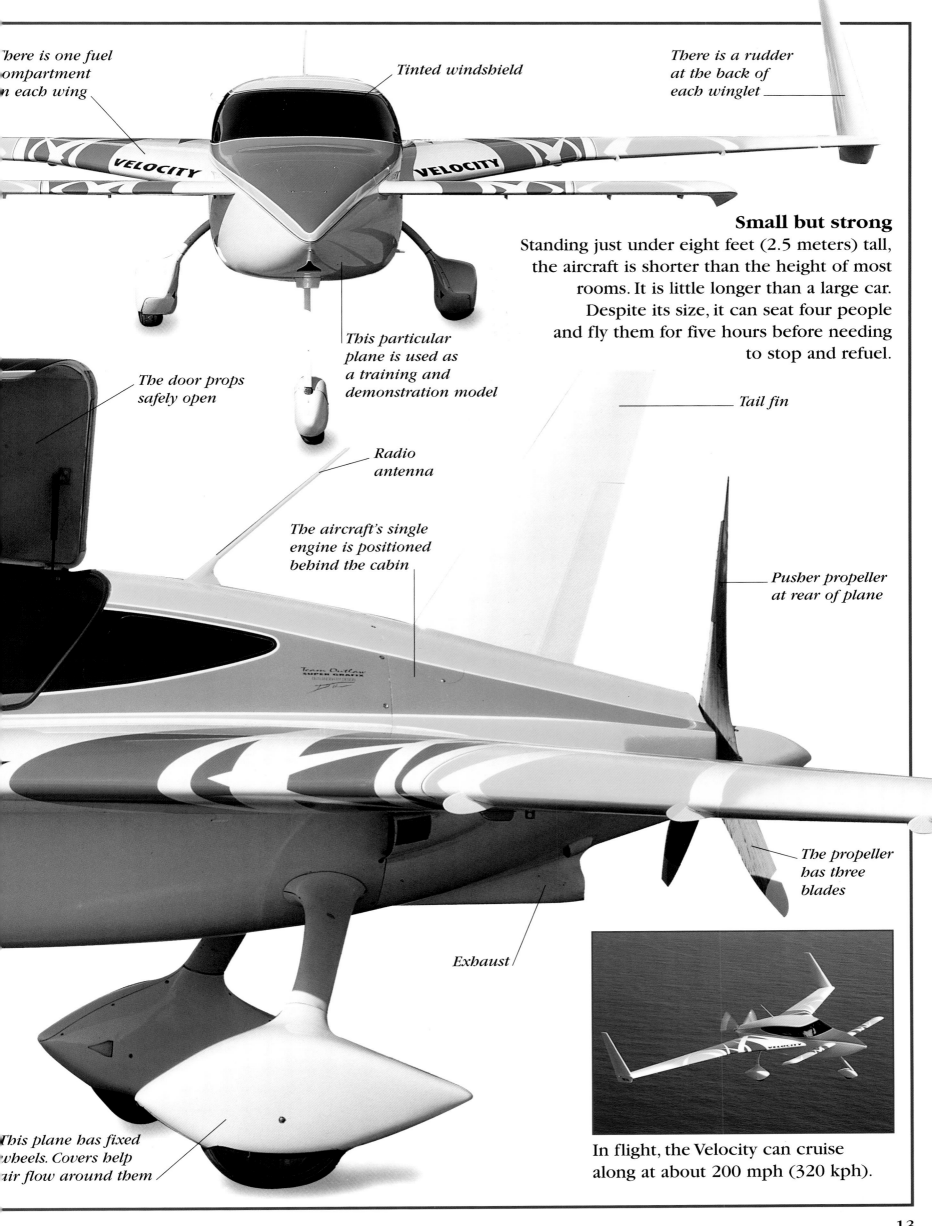

There is one fuel compartment in each wing

Tinted windshield

There is a rudder at the back of each winglet

Small but strong

Standing just under eight feet (2.5 meters) tall, the aircraft is shorter than the height of most rooms. It is little longer than a large car. Despite its size, it can seat four people and fly them for five hours before needing to stop and refuel.

The door props safely open

This particular plane is used as a training and demonstration model

Tail fin

Radio antenna

The aircraft's single engine is positioned behind the cabin

Pusher propeller at rear of plane

The propeller has three blades

Exhaust

This plane has fixed wheels. Covers help air flow around them

In flight, the Velocity can cruise along at about 200 mph (320 kph).

Stunt planes

Go to an air show and you'll see brightly colored planes zipping past, wing tips almost touching. Watch as highly trained pilots take the planes into intricate loops, rolls, and flips. It's an exciting sight when the stunt planes perform incredible air acrobatics.

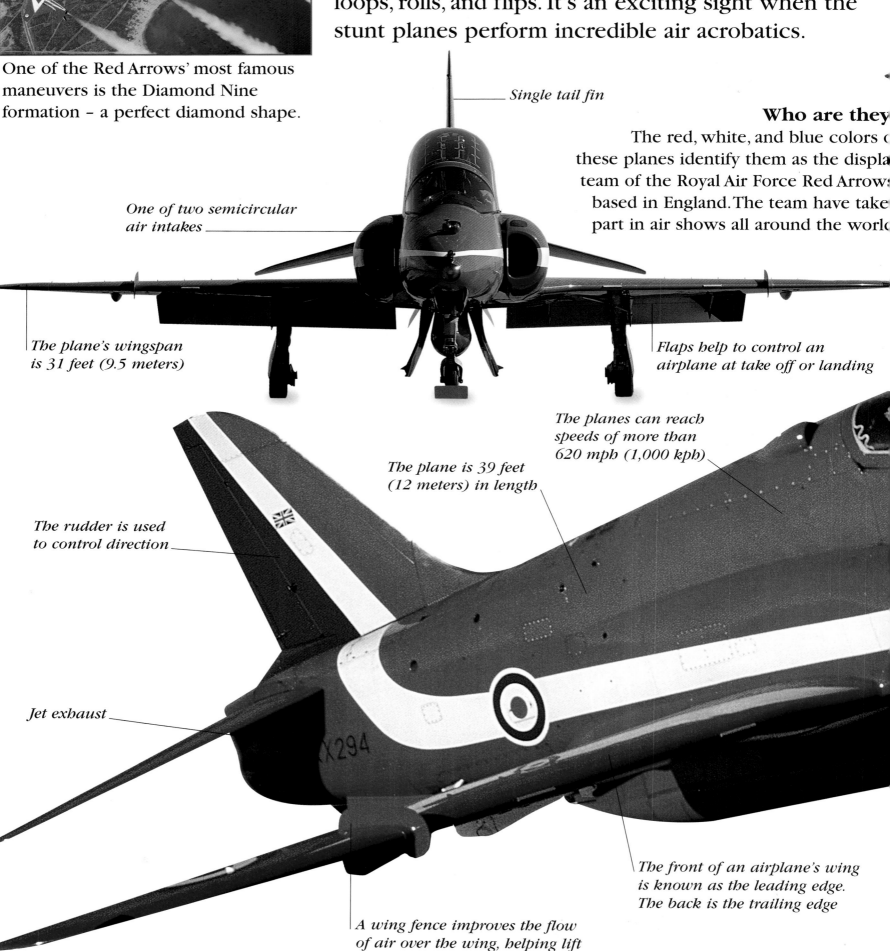

One of the Red Arrows' most famous maneuvers is the Diamond Nine formation – a perfect diamond shape.

Single tail fin

Who are they

The red, white, and blue colors these planes identify them as the displa team of the Royal Air Force Red Arrow based in England. The team have take part in air shows all around the worl

One of two semicircular air intakes

The plane's wingspan is 31 feet (9.5 meters)

Flaps help to control an airplane at take off or landing

The planes can reach speeds of more than 620 mph (1,000 kph)

The plane is 39 feet (12 meters) in length

The rudder is used to control direction

Jet exhaust

XX294

The front of an airplane's wing is known as the leading edge. The back is the trailing edge

A wing fence improves the flow of air over the wing, helping lift

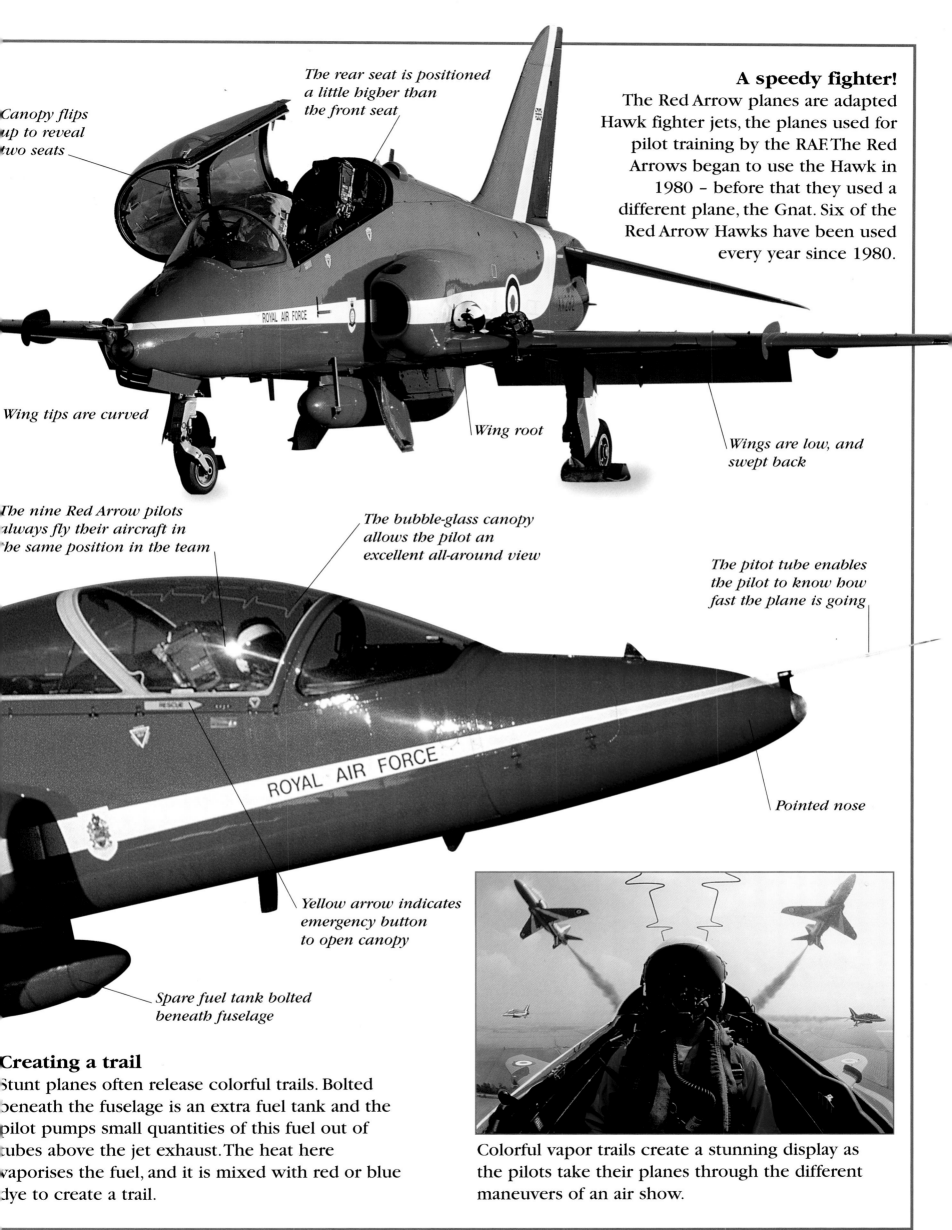

The rear seat is positioned
a little higher than
the front seat

Canopy flips
up to reveal
two seats

A speedy fighter!
The Red Arrow planes are adapted
Hawk fighter jets, the planes used for
pilot training by the RAF. The Red
Arrows began to use the Hawk in
1980 – before that they used a
different plane, the Gnat. Six of the
Red Arrow Hawks have been used
every year since 1980.

Wing tips are curved

Wing root

Wings are low, and
swept back

The nine Red Arrow pilots
always fly their aircraft in
the same position in the team

The bubble-glass canopy
allows the pilot an
excellent all-around view

The pitot tube enables
the pilot to know how
fast the plane is going

ROYAL AIR FORCE

Pointed nose

Yellow arrow indicates
emergency button
to open canopy

Spare fuel tank bolted
beneath fuselage

Creating a trail
Stunt planes often release colorful trails. Bolted
beneath the fuselage is an extra fuel tank and the
pilot pumps small quantities of this fuel out of
tubes above the jet exhaust. The heat here
vaporises the fuel, and it is mixed with red or blue
dye to create a trail.

Colorful vapor trails create a stunning display as
the pilots take their planes through the different
maneuvers of an air show.

Flying laboratory

The ER-2 has four compartments that hold experiments. One is in the fuselage, one is in the nose, and two are in pods that can be attached to the wings.

This unusual looking long-nosed plane is designed to cruise at altitudes of about 13.5 miles (22 km). That's more than twice the cruising altitude of a jumbo jet! It needs to do this because it is a flying science aircraft, or flying laboratory, specially equipped to collect information about the Earth. Its official name is the ER-2.

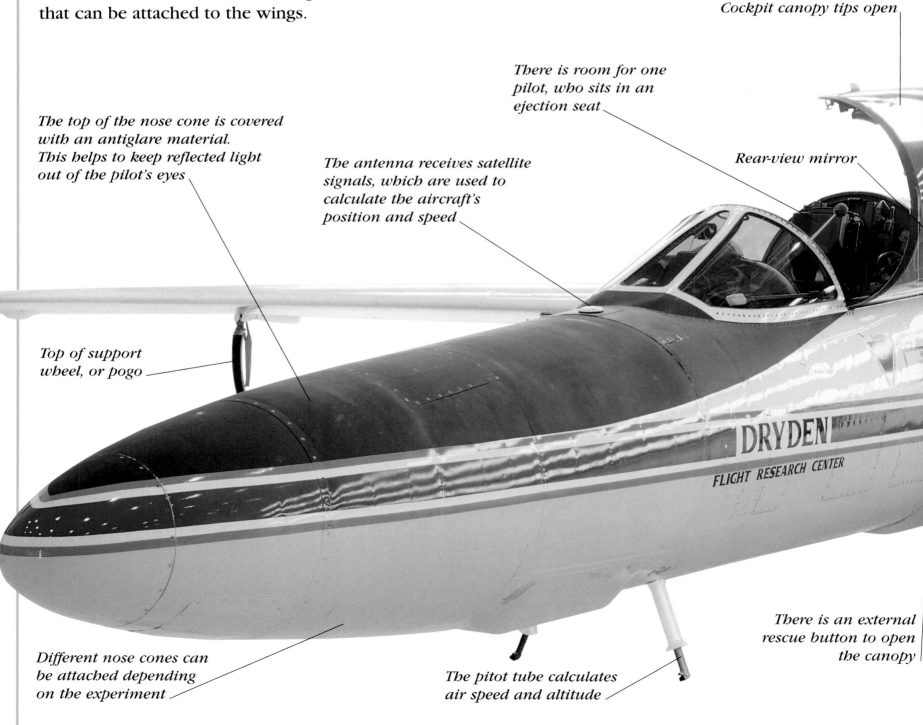

Cockpit canopy tips open

There is room for one pilot, who sits in an ejection seat

Rear-view mirror

The top of the nose cone is covered with an antiglare material. This helps to keep reflected light out of the pilot's eyes

The antenna receives satellite signals, which are used to calculate the aircraft's position and speed

Top of support wheel, or pogo

There is an external rescue button to open the canopy

Different nose cones can be attached depending on the experiment

The pitot tube calculates air speed and altitude

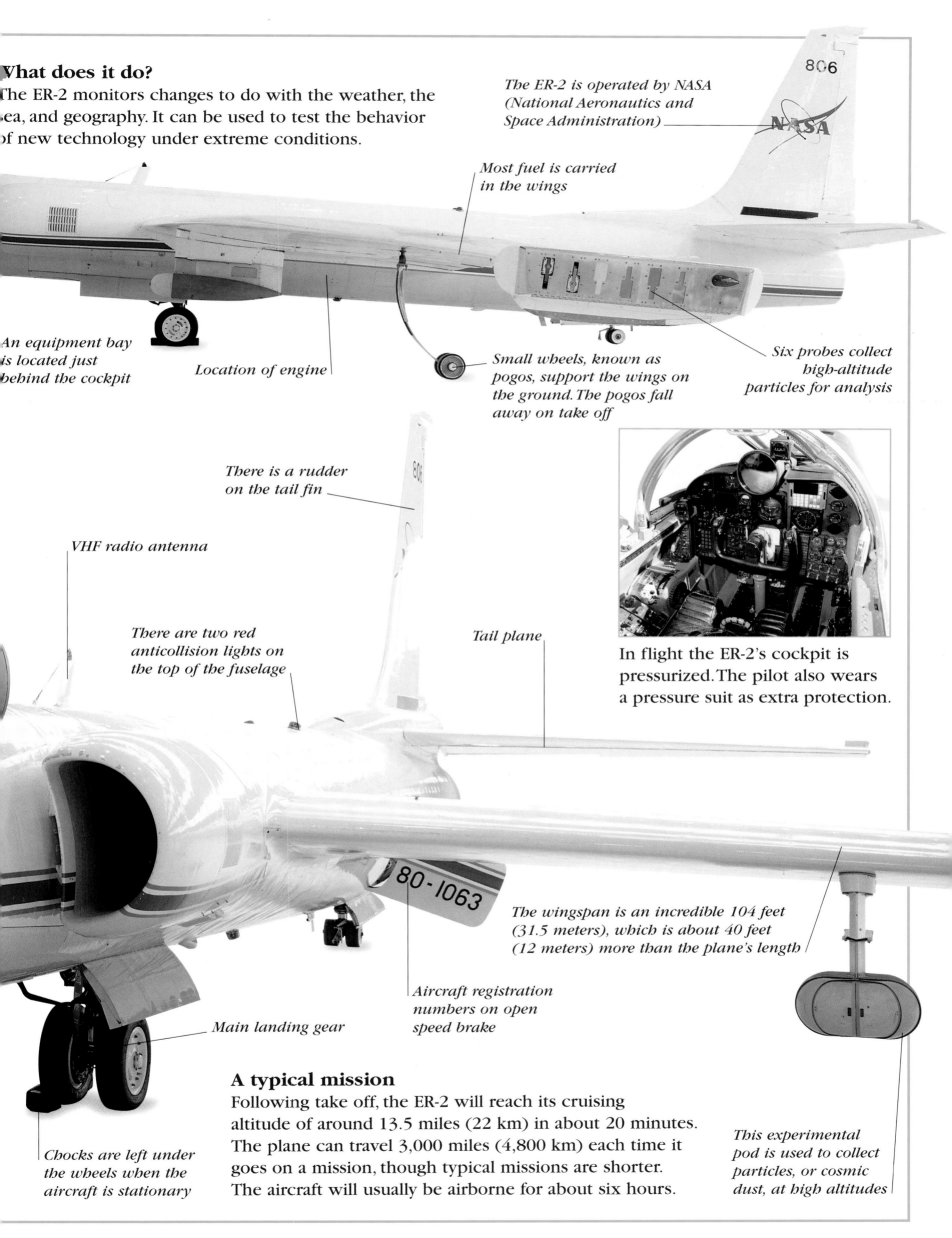

What does it do?

The ER-2 monitors changes to do with the weather, the sea, and geography. It can be used to test the behavior of new technology under extreme conditions.

The ER-2 is operated by NASA (National Aeronautics and Space Administration)

806

NASA

Most fuel is carried in the wings

An equipment bay is located just behind the cockpit

Location of engine

Small wheels, known as pogos, support the wings on the ground. The pogos fall away on take off

Six probes collect high-altitude particles for analysis

There is a rudder on the tail fin

VHF radio antenna

There are two red anticollision lights on the top of the fuselage

Tail plane

In flight the ER-2's cockpit is pressurized. The pilot also wears a pressure suit as extra protection.

80-1063

Main landing gear

Aircraft registration numbers on open speed brake

The wingspan is an incredible 104 feet (31.5 meters), which is about 40 feet (12 meters) more than the plane's length

A typical mission

Following take off, the ER-2 will reach its cruising altitude of around 13.5 miles (22 km) in about 20 minutes. The plane can travel 3,000 miles (4,800 km) each time it goes on a mission, though typical missions are shorter. The aircraft will usually be airborne for about six hours.

Chocks are left under the wheels when the aircraft is stationary

This experimental pod is used to collect particles, or cosmic dust, at high altitudes

Ultralight

Although it looks small, this ultralight can stay in the air for up to four hours, burning up fuel at the rate of three gallons (13.5 liters) per hour. Many ultralight pilots take part in competitions, carrying out a series of tasks such as photographing things on the ground, or switching off the engine before landing. It is an exciting sport.

Ultralights usually fly at about 3,000 feet (900 meters) – a jumbo jet flies at ten times that height.

This zipper is opened during the preflight inspection to allow the pilot to check that the cables are correctly connected

Battens hold the wing material taut

A safe flight

Before an ultralight pilot can take off, he or she will check over the aircraft, just like a pilot does for a larger plane. The pilot walks around the ultralight, checking that the controls are rigged correctly, the wing is properly secured to the body, the tires are okay, and also testing the engine and the exhaust. This can take about 20 minutes.

The wing is often referred to as a sail – the material is similar to that used for yacht sails

Rigging lines strengthen the ultralight

Like airplanes, ultralights have to be registered with the aircraft authority of the country in which they are flown

The ultralight's wingspan is just over 33 feet (ten meters)

Twenty-nine battens run through the wing

The battens are secured in place with elastic cord

Push-to-talk button for radio

Spats cover wheels to decrease air resistance

The tires are filled to a slightly lower pressure than a motorcycle's tires, making them softer. This cushions the ultralight on landing

Keep in touch

When in the air, the pilot ca contact air-traffic control or peopl on the ground at the flight strip b using a simple radio. The radi connection clips to the control ba

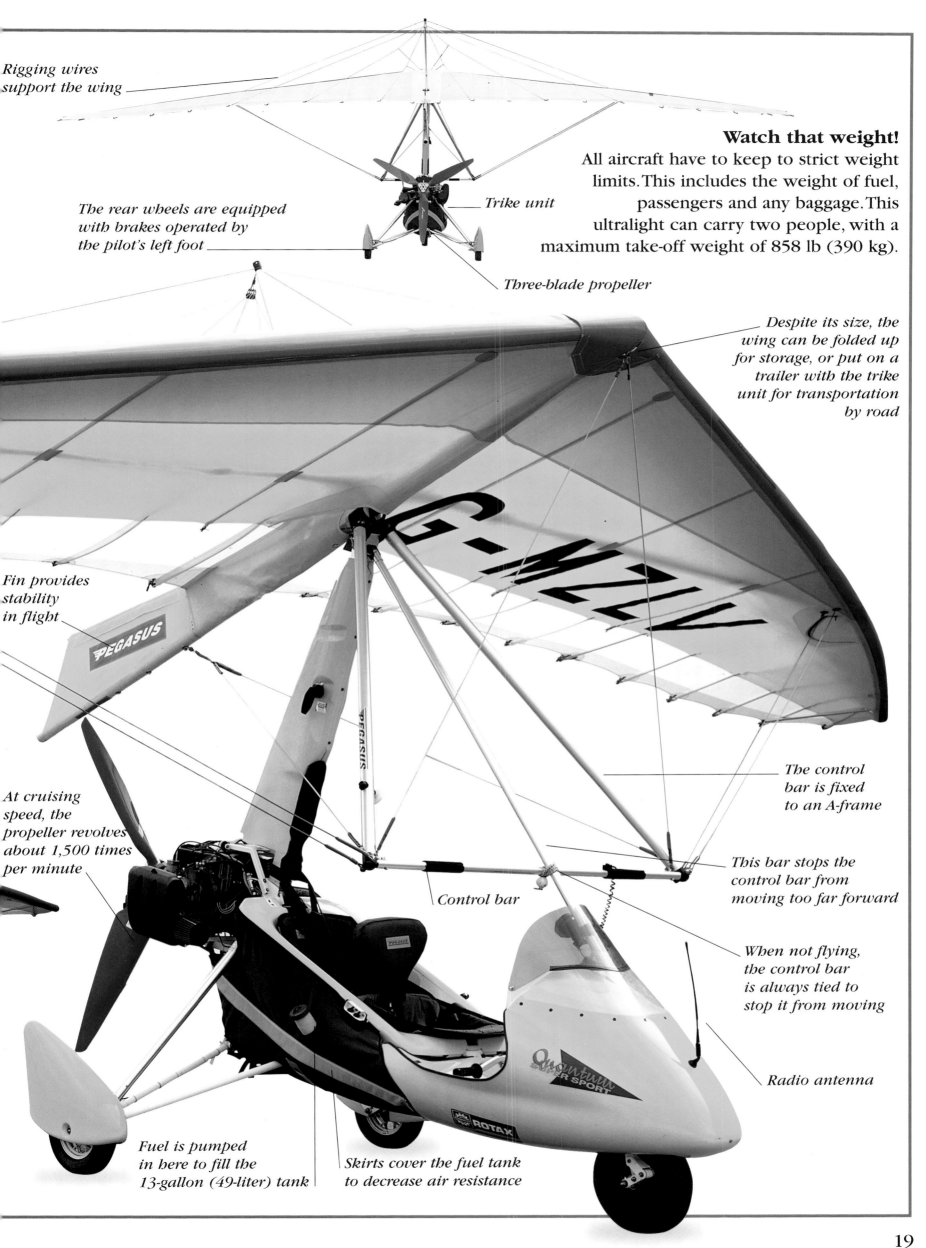

Rigging wires
support the wing

The rear wheels are equipped
with brakes operated by
the pilot's left foot

Trike unit

Watch that weight!
All aircraft have to keep to strict weight
limits. This includes the weight of fuel,
passengers and any baggage. This
ultralight can carry two people, with a
maximum take-off weight of 858 lb (390 kg).

Three-blade propeller

Despite its size, the
wing can be folded up
for storage, or put on a
trailer with the trike
unit for transportation
by road

Fin provides
stability
in flight

PEGASUS

G-MZLV

PEGASUS

At cruising
speed, the
propeller revolves
about 1,500 times
per minute

The control
bar is fixed
to an A-frame

Control bar

This bar stops the
control bar from
moving too far forward

When not flying,
the control bar
is always tied to
stop it from moving

Radio antenna

Quantum
SUPER SPORT

ROTAX

Fuel is pumped
in here to fill the
13-gallon (49-liter) tank

Skirts cover the fuel tank
to decrease air resistance

19

The Concorde

With its swept-back wings, sleek shape, and drooping nose, the Concorde is a familiar sight. It is a supersonic airplane, capable of cruising at more than twice the speed of sound. A record flight saw it crossing the Atlantic from New York to London in just under three hours – less than half the time a jumbo jet takes. It also cruises along at about twice the altitude of a jumbo, which means that its passengers can see the curve of the Earth.

The Concorde's top speed is 1,430 mph (2,300 kph)

Fuel is carried in huge tanks in the wings

At take off, Concorde is traveling at 250 mph (402 kph)

Once in the air, the Concorde guzzles fuel at the rate of 111 gallons (427 liters) each minute. It can travel about 3,740 miles (5,900 km) without stopping to refuel, and flies at an altitude of about 10 miles (16 km), which is too high to be affected by air turbulance.

The wingspan is less than half that of a jumbo jet

Aerodynamic strake directs airflow around cockpit area

The Concorde's nose can be straightened, or dropped down

Passengers enter through this door

VHF antenna

Emergency exit

Retractable visor

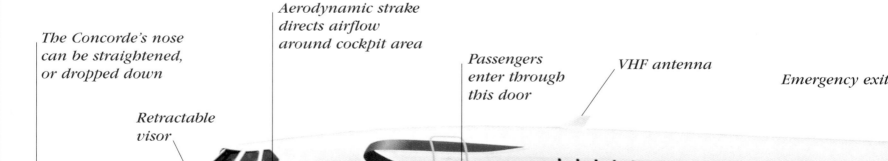

BRITISH AIRWAYS

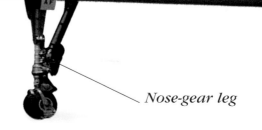

Nose-gear leg

A moveable nose

The Concorde's nose straightens out when the plane is flying. This helps the plane to cut through the air. It drops down for take off and landing, so that the pilot has a better view of the runway. The nose contains radar equipment.

Crossing the speed of sound

When an airplane crosses the speed of sound, it produces a sound known as a sonic boom. It's a loud noise a bit like a clap of thunder. It happens because the plane is breaking through the sound waves it has been pushing ahead of it. The passengers don't really feel anything, and they cannot hear the boom – it's heard from the ground.

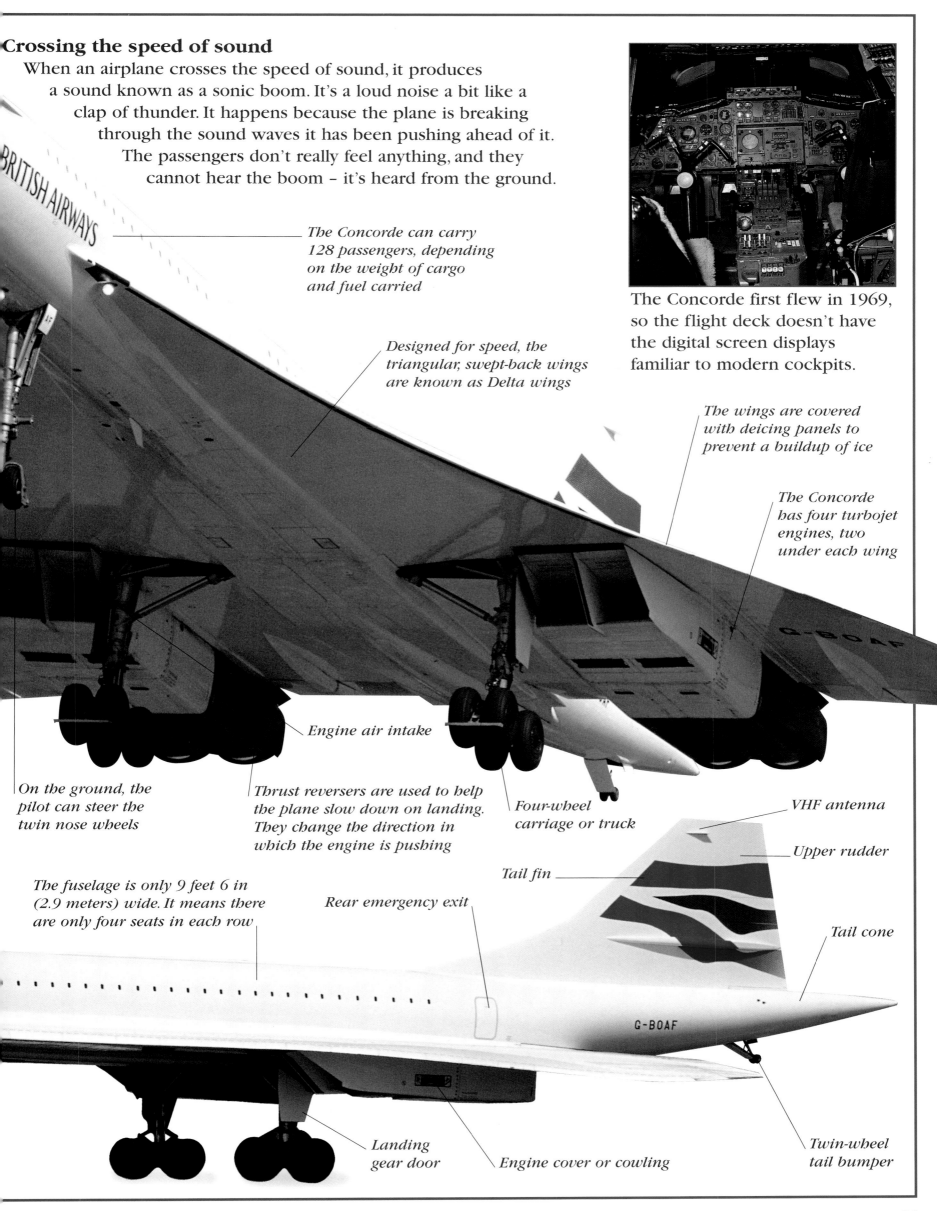

The Concorde first flew in 1969, so the flight deck doesn't have the digital screen displays familiar to modern cockpits.

The Concorde can carry 128 passengers, depending on the weight of cargo and fuel carried

Designed for speed, the triangular, swept-back wings are known as Delta wings

The wings are covered with deicing panels to prevent a buildup of ice

The Concorde has four turbojet engines, two under each wing

Engine air intake

On the ground, the pilot can steer the twin nose wheels

Thrust reversers are used to help the plane slow down on landing. They change the direction in which the engine is pushing

Four-wheel carriage or truck

VHF antenna

Upper rudder

Tail fin

Tail cone

The fuselage is only 9 feet 6 in (2.9 meters) wide. It means there are only four seats in each row

Rear emergency exit

Landing gear door

Engine cover or cowling

Twin-wheel tail bumper

21

Blackbird (SR-71A)

The Blackbird, or SR-71A, is a perfect spy plane. Not only can it fly at a jaw-dropping 2,000 mph (3,218 kph) – that's more than three times the speed of sound – its onboard cameras can read a license plate on a car from 17 miles (27 km) up! Now rarely used, the plane was first flown in the US in 1964.

On the way up, fuel streaks out. The plane's fuel tanks leak until they expand and seal as a result of high temperatures caused by speed.

Red ribbons clearly indicate protective covers that have to be removed before take off

The whole rudder moves on a hinge at the base

Food is carried in tubes. The crew hold the tubes against the cockpit glass to warm the food!

The SR-71A carries a crew of two – a pilot and a reconnaissance systems officer

A curved edge, known as a chine, provides lift and stability to the front of the aircraft

Circular air intake (protected when on the ground) supplies air to the engine

Cone pulls back 26 in (66 cm) in flight, controlling the air allowed into the engine

Fuel more than doubles the empty weight of the plane

Landing lights

Smash those records!
The Blackbird is the fastest jet-engine aircraft in the world. It set a number of world speed records in 1976, reaching 2,193 mph (3,530 kph). It also set an altitude record for a jet-engine aircraft of 85,069 feet (25,930 meters).

Front landing gear

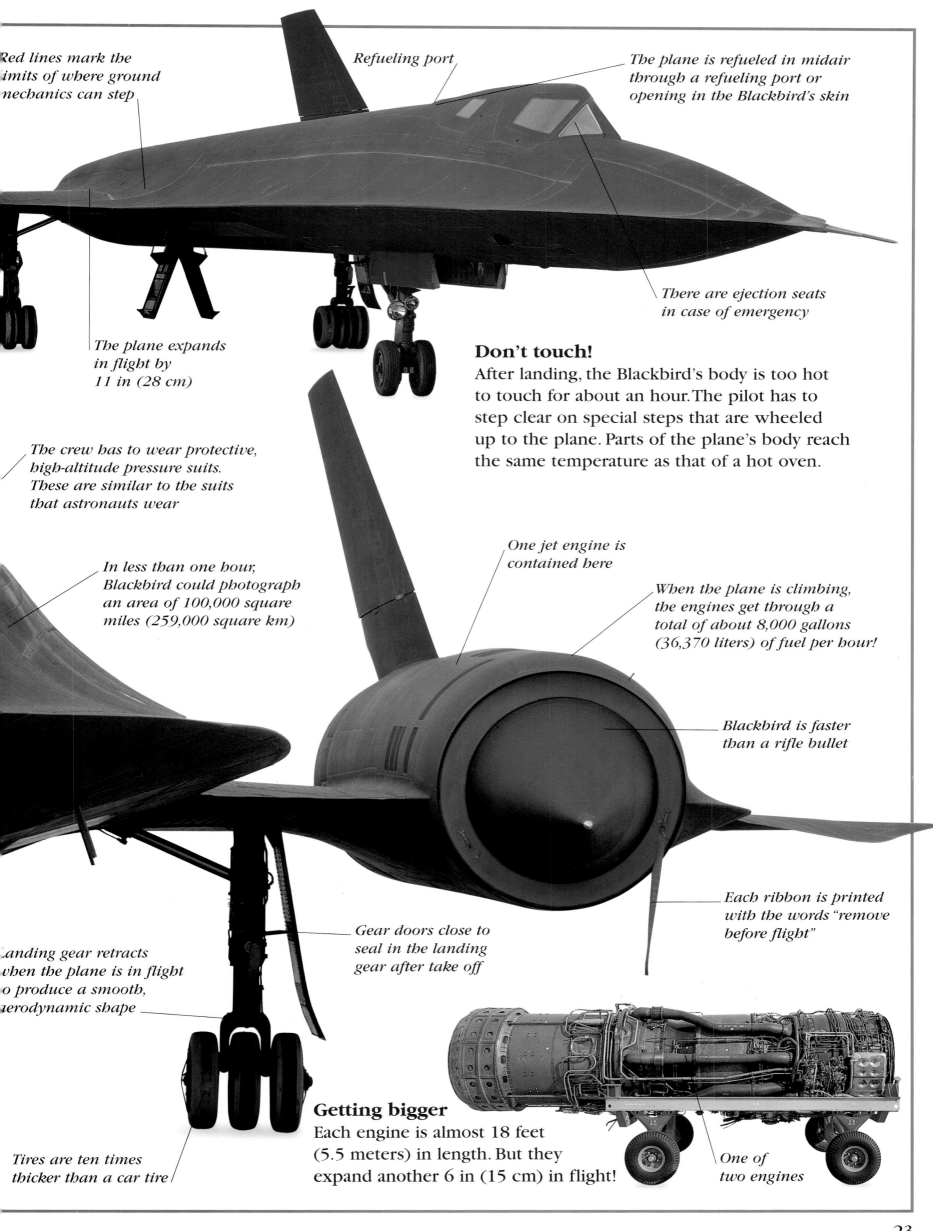

Red lines mark the limits of where ground mechanics can step

Refueling port

The plane is refueled in midair through a refueling port or opening in the Blackbird's skin

There are ejection seats in case of emergency

The plane expands in flight by 11 in (28 cm)

The crew has to wear protective, high-altitude pressure suits. These are similar to the suits that astronauts wear

In less than one hour, Blackbird could photograph an area of 100,000 square miles (259,000 square km)

Don't touch!

After landing, the Blackbird's body is too hot to touch for about an hour. The pilot has to step clear on special steps that are wheeled up to the plane. Parts of the plane's body reach the same temperature as that of a hot oven.

One jet engine is contained here

When the plane is climbing, the engines get through a total of about 8,000 gallons (36,370 liters) of fuel per hour!

Blackbird is faster than a rifle bullet

Each ribbon is printed with the words "remove before flight"

Landing gear retracts when the plane is in flight to produce a smooth, aerodynamic shape

Gear doors close to seal in the landing gear after take off

Tires are ten times thicker than a car tire

Getting bigger

Each engine is almost 18 feet (5.5 meters) in length. But they expand another 6 in (15 cm) in flight!

One of two engines

Chinook helicopter

A helicopter can hover and pick up a load from a very restricted space. It might be lifting logs from a heavily wooded hillside or transporting huge pipes. This Chinook helicopter is unusually powerful. It has been stripped of unnecessary equipment to make it lighter so that it can lift more than its own weight in cargo. It is known as a utility Chinook.

The hefty steel cable used to lift loads is one inch (2.5 cm) thick and 200 feet (60 meters) long.

The blades spin around at 225 times per minute

A thirst for fuel

Helicopter engines burn up a lot of fuel spinning the rotors to lift the machine up. During routine heavy-lift operations, this Chinook uses 333 gallons (1,515 liters) of fuel per hour. It is typically refueled every 1½ hours.

Each rotor blade is 30 feet (nine meters) in length

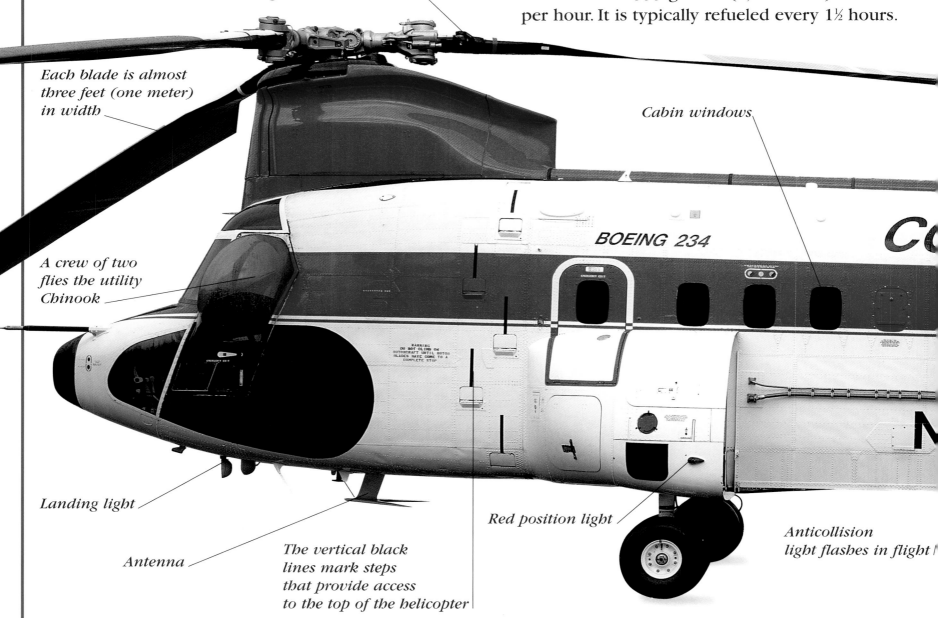

Each blade is almost three feet (one meter) in width

Cabin windows

A crew of two flies the utility Chinook

BOEING 234

CO

M

Landing light

Red position light

Anticollision light flashes in flight

Antenna

The vertical black lines mark steps that provide access to the top of the helicopter

Flight control

A pilot works with a copilot, so the cockpit controls are the same on both sides. Both pilot and copilot have more than 150 control buttons and switches around them.

The blades droop when the Chinook is on the ground

Bubble windows provide the pilot with excellent visibility of the load below

It is a US Forest Service requirement that the tops of the blades are yellow and white

The inside is empty of seats to keep weight low. A car could fit into the space left behind.

There are almost 80,000 moving parts on the helicopter

The fore and aft rotor blades interweave as they spin to lift the helicopter into the air

One of two turbine engines

A screen stops small things from hitting the engine

Emergency exit door

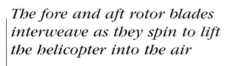

Fuel line to pump fuel to engines

External cargo hook

Steerable landing gear

A military Chinook has a rear cargo access ramp, but this has been removed from the utility Chinook as it is unnecessary and would add unwanted weight

Seaplane

Seaplanes are useful in areas where there are large natural harbors and lots of lakes and mountains. They are basically planes that have floats instead of wheels, so they are unable to land on a runway. Instead, they land on and take off from water.

Green starboard light

Which side is which?

At night it can be difficult to tell which way a plane is facing. To solve this problem, airplanes, like boats, have red port lights on the left and green starboard lights on the right.

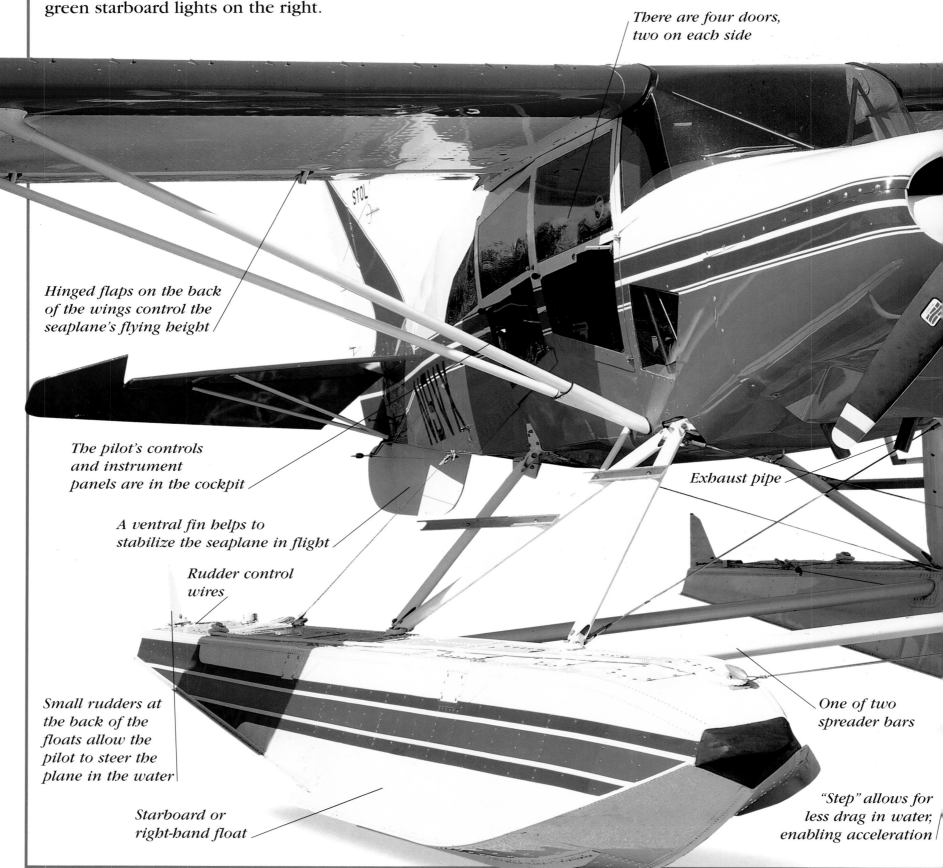

There are four doors, two on each side

Hinged flaps on the back of the wings control the seaplane's flying height

The pilot's controls and instrument panels are in the cockpit

A ventral fin helps to stabilize the seaplane in flight

Rudder control wires

Exhaust pipe

Small rudders at the back of the floats allow the pilot to steer the plane in the water

Starboard or right-hand float

One of two spreader bars

"Step" allows for less drag in water, enabling acceleration

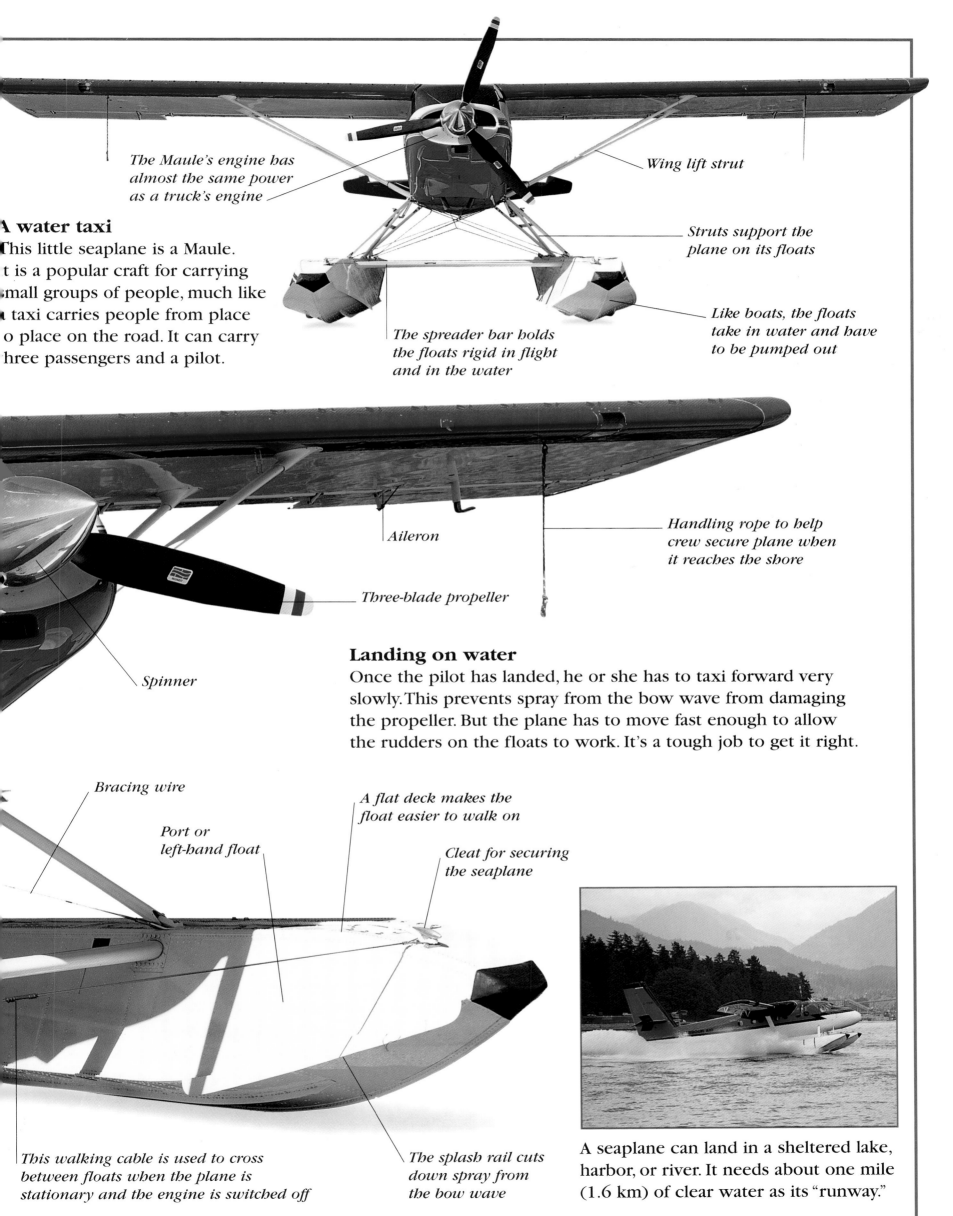

The Maule's engine has almost the same power as a truck's engine

Wing lift strut

Struts support the plane on its floats

A water taxi

This little seaplane is a Maule. It is a popular craft for carrying small groups of people, much like a taxi carries people from place to place on the road. It can carry three passengers and a pilot.

The spreader bar holds the floats rigid in flight and in the water

Like boats, the floats take in water and have to be pumped out

Aileron

Handling rope to help crew secure plane when it reaches the shore

Three-blade propeller

Spinner

Landing on water

Once the pilot has landed, he or she has to taxi forward very slowly. This prevents spray from the bow wave from damaging the propeller. But the plane has to move fast enough to allow the rudders on the floats to work. It's a tough job to get it right.

Bracing wire

A flat deck makes the float easier to walk on

Port or left-hand float

Cleat for securing the seaplane

This walking cable is used to cross between floats when the plane is stationary and the engine is switched off

The splash rail cuts down spray from the bow wave

A seaplane can land in a sheltered lake, harbor, or river. It needs about one mile (1.6 km) of clear water as its "runway."

F-16

Raised canopy

Instructor pilot

Trainee pilot

RESCUE

FORCE

Forward landing gear

Pitot tube

The F-16 is a multi-role fighter aircraft, originally designed for close-up air combat. It is also used for air-to-ground attack. It has excellent maneuverability. Flying at a height of 7.5 miles (12 km), an F-16 can reach a speed of 1,350 mph (2,172 kph), or just over twice the speed of sound. The F-16 is officially known as the Fighting Falcon, but all the pilots call it the Viper.

This specially adapted pitot tube is only used for flight tests

Getting ready to go

The pilots and ground crew have lots of checks to complete before they are ready to take off. These take them about 45 minutes – they check everything, including the flight controls.

The cockpit is equipped with a visual display screen known as a Heads-Up-Display. It tells the pilots where they are and displays weapons and targeting information

MAJ. ROB ADAM

RESCUE

A bright yellow arrow points to a handle. Ground personnel pull this to jettison the canopy in an emergency

The first F-16s had black radomes (or radar covers). Pilots felt it was an easy target for enemy fire, so the black was changed to gray

The forward landing gear retracts into a compartment in flight

The F-16 is the most commonly flown aircraft in the US Air Force. It is also used in many other countries.

The F-16 has a unique flight control system known as fly-by-wire. It means that computers and electronics have replaced many of the older-style mechanical workings

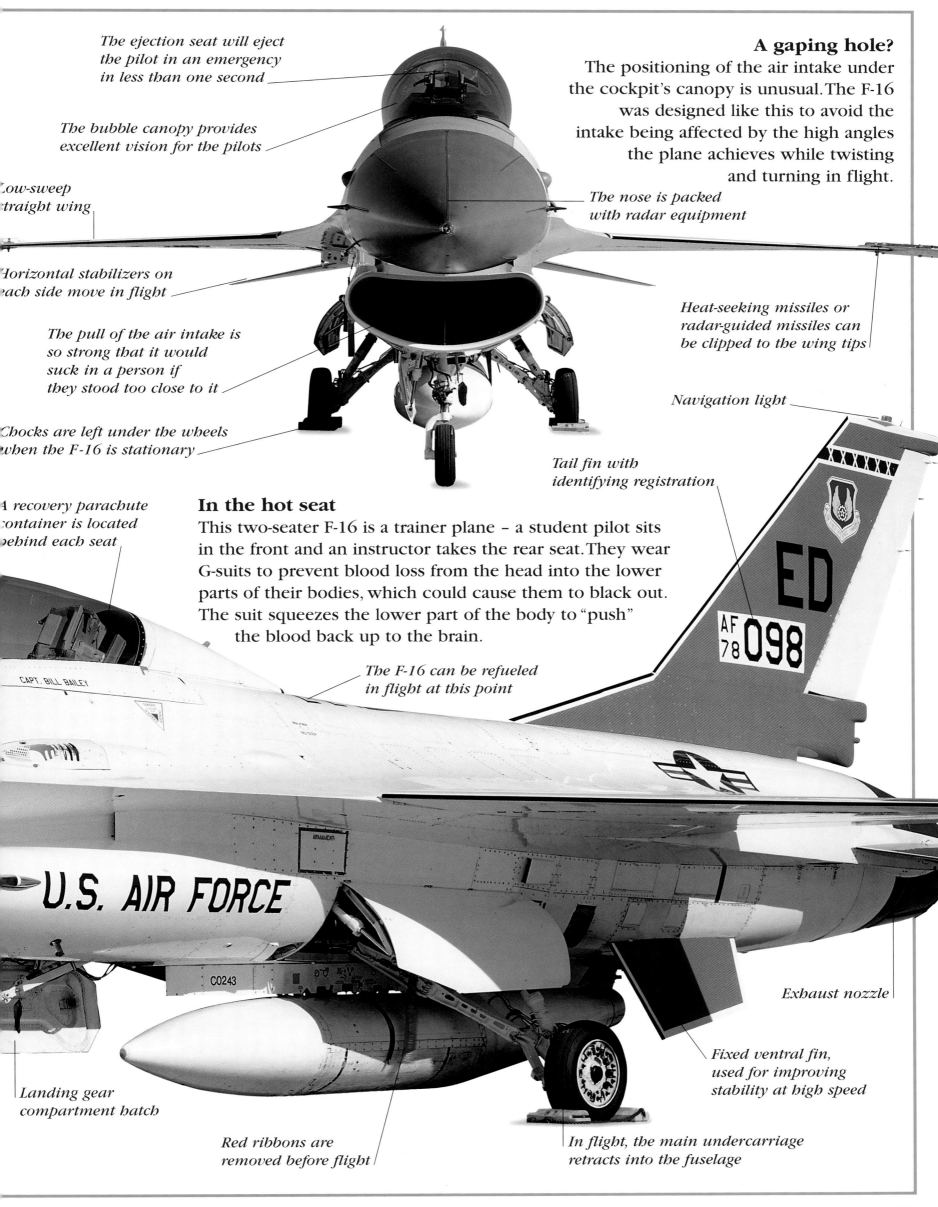

The ejection seat will eject the pilot in an emergency in less than one second

The bubble canopy provides excellent vision for the pilots

Low-sweep straight wing

Horizontal stabilizers on each side move in flight

The pull of the air intake is so strong that it would suck in a person if they stood too close to it

Chocks are left under the wheels when the F-16 is stationary

A recovery parachute container is located behind each seat

A gaping hole?
The positioning of the air intake under the cockpit's canopy is unusual. The F-16 was designed like this to avoid the intake being affected by the high angles the plane achieves while twisting and turning in flight.

The nose is packed with radar equipment

Heat-seeking missiles or radar-guided missiles can be clipped to the wing tips

Navigation light

Tail fin with identifying registration

In the hot seat
This two-seater F-16 is a trainer plane – a student pilot sits in the front and an instructor takes the rear seat. They wear G-suits to prevent blood loss from the head into the lower parts of their bodies, which could cause them to black out. The suit squeezes the lower part of the body to "push" the blood back up to the brain.

The F-16 can be refueled in flight at this point

ED

AF 78 098

CAPT. BILL BAILEY

U.S. AIR FORCE

C0243

Exhaust nozzle

Fixed ventral fin, used for improving stability at high speed

Landing gear compartment hatch

Red ribbons are removed before flight

In flight, the main undercarriage retracts into the fuselage

Space flight

The space shuttle is now a familiar sight as it blasts into space on the back of its huge fuel tank. It is used to launch and repair space satellites, but this is costly, partly because the fuel tank is discarded after each mission. A fully reusable craft with internal fuel tanks would be a cheaper alternative – and one is currently being developed. This wedge-shaped space plane is the X-33, a reusable launch vehicle.

The space shuttle is launched on the back of a huge fuel tank and two booster rockets.

Vertical stabilizer

The two engines are located at the back of the space plane

The horizontal fins are coated with ceramic tiles to protect them from high temperatures

One of the two liquid hydrogen tanks is located here

A "strong back" lifts the X-33 to a vertical postion

A movable hangar positioned on rails will protect the X-33 when it is being serviced between flights

There are more than 1,300 black metal plates, known as thermal protection panels, on the X-33's nose and lower surface

A flame trench directs exhaust following launch away from the base of the X-33

At the launch pad

The X-33 will be fueled and launched vertically from a specially built launch pad. It will shoot up at speeds of more than Mach 13 (13 times the speed of sound or about 10,000 mph [16,000 kph]) and then glide back to land like an airplane.

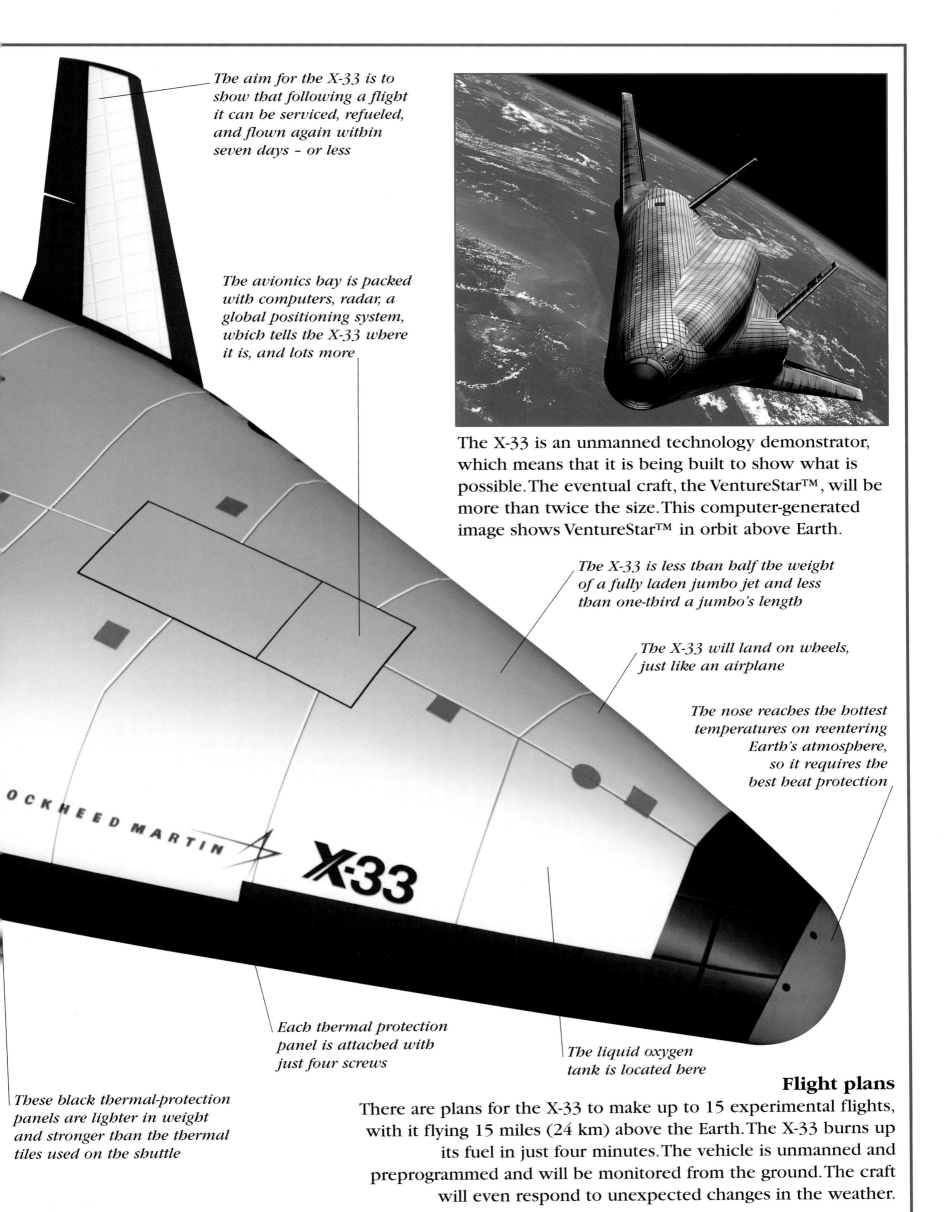

The aim for the X-33 is to show that following a flight it can be serviced, refueled, and flown again within seven days – or less

The avionics bay is packed with computers, radar, a global positioning system, which tells the X-33 where it is, and lots more

The X-33 is an unmanned technology demonstrator, which means that it is being built to show what is possible. The eventual craft, the VentureStar™, will be more than twice the size. This computer-generated image shows VentureStar™ in orbit above Earth.

The X-33 is less than half the weight of a fully laden jumbo jet and less than one-third a jumbo's length

The X-33 will land on wheels, just like an airplane

The nose reaches the hottest temperatures on reentering Earth's atmosphere, so it requires the best heat protection

OCKHEED MARTIN

X-33

Each thermal protection panel is attached with just four screws

The liquid oxygen tank is located here

These black thermal-protection panels are lighter in weight and stronger than the thermal tiles used on the shuttle

Flight plans

There are plans for the X-33 to make up to 15 experimental flights, with it flying 15 miles (24 km) above the Earth. The X-33 burns up its fuel in just four minutes. The vehicle is unmanned and preprogrammed and will be monitored from the ground. The craft will even respond to unexpected changes in the weather.

Glossary

Aerodynamic
A shape designed to cut through air with the least resistance possible.

Aileron
A flap close to a plane's wing tip that is used to control roll.

Air intake
The place where air is taken into a machine. Air is needed to mix with fuel to make an engine go.

Altitude
The height of an object.

Antenna
A wire or rod that protrudes from an object to pick up radio waves.

Avionics
An aircraft's electronic and navigation equipment.

Ejection seat
A seat that contains an explosive charge and a parachute. It can be ejected from an airplane in an emergency to save the pilot.

Elevator
Flat control surfaces that are used to make a plane climb or dive.

Exhaust
The pipe through which waste fumes are expelled from an engine.

Fuselage
The body of an aircraft.

Horsepower
The measure of an engine's power. One unit of horsepower is loosely based on the power of a horse.

Hypersonic
A plane traveling at more than five times the speed of sound.

Jet engine
All engines need fuel and oxygen to make them go. A jet engine gulps the oxygen it needs from the air around it.

Landing gear
The wheels of an airplane.

Mph/kph
These letters stand for miles per hour and kilometers per hour, measurements of an object's speed.

Pitot tube
A pipe that protrudes from an aircraft and measures air speed.

Port
A ship or airplane's left-hand side.

Radar
A means of detecting objects that are not within sight.

Rocket engine
A rocket engine carries the oxygen it needs in a tank. See also Jet engine.

Rudder
A hinged flap that is used to turn an aircraft to the left or right.

Speed of sound
This varies depending on air temperature, which is affected by altitude. At sea level, sound travels at about 760 mph (1,224 kph).

Starboard
A ship or airplane's right-hand side.

Thermal protection
An external coating or covering that protects an airplane from excessive heat.

Undercarriage
An aircraft's landing gear.

Index